HOW
TO FIND

Calm

SOPHIE GOLDING

HOW TO FIND CALM

An Hachette UK Company
www.hachette.co.uk

Vie Books, an imprint of Summersdale Publishers Ltd
Part of Octopus Publishing Group Limited
Carmelite House
50 Victoria Embankment
LONDON
EC4Y 0DZ
UK

www.summersdale.com

Printed and bound in China

ISBN: 978-1-78685-994-5

Substantial discounts on bulk quantities of Summersdale books are available to corporations, professional associations and other organizations. For details contact general enquiries: telephone: +44 (0)1243 771107 or email: enquiries@summersdale.com.

CONTENTS

INTRODUCTION

Do you find yourself racing anxiously through each day? Perhaps you don't feel you have time to focus on your own needs? Or maybe you end up feeling so wired each evening that you struggle to sleep? If this resonates with you, it could be time to start nourishing your own mental, physical, emotional and spiritual well-being. The following pages contain a selection of calming, easy-to-follow tips, practical advice and inspiring quotes to help introduce a deeper sense of peace into your life.

The Power of Your Mind

YOUR MIND IS A POWERFUL TOOL

The average human brain contains approximately 100 billion neurons, which work together to create more than 100 trillion connections. Yet, despite (or perhaps because of) the brain's complexity, many people encounter a common dilemma: we can get so caught up in our ability to interpret and process multiple scenarios and problems that we have difficulty noticing the silence – the silence behind our cognition, behind our constant internal dialogue and behind the tangle of automatic thoughts that can disrupt our inner peace. Learning how to move beyond the noise of the mind and enter that quiet space can help to restore your inner calm in an increasingly chaotic world.

AUTOMATIC THINKING

We have perhaps as many as 70,000 thoughts every day. That's a lot of thinking – and much of it is automatic. The first step to finding calm is recognizing that these thoughts are not facts: they are simply your mind attempting to interpret the world around you. Because of this, you don't have to believe everything you think. A weight will lift from your shoulders the moment you truly know this.

NOTICE THE SILENCE BEHIND YOUR INNER VOICE.

ESCAPE MIND TRAPS

A mind trap is a repetitive thought pattern that can lead you into a state of anxiety – for example, constantly worrying about an upcoming event. By noticing this cycle and then reframing your thoughts, you can put a stop to the mind trap that's ruining your peace of mind. Next time you notice yourself stuck in a cycle of negative thoughts, do something physical to interrupt the pattern: hum a song or stamp your feet – anything you like. This physical distraction can give you a brief moment to mentally pause and "switch off" the cycle, before you consciously think about something else.

Your calm mind is the ultimate weapon against your challenges. So relax.

Bryant McGill

REALIZE YOU ARE NOT YOUR THOUGHTS

This is a powerful realization and one that can be deeply calming. To begin, spend a little time noticing your thoughts. Really listen to that voice in your head. What is it saying? Often, it will be interpreting situations or simply narrating – detailing everything you see or hear, as well as chattering away about things you need to do or remember. It might be voicing your worries. It is constant – and it can become draining. Noticing this inner voice gives you the opportunity to step back from it. From this place of distance, it's easier to accept the following: if you can notice your thoughts, then it means that you are not your thoughts. Every time your thoughts start to overwhelm you – or your inner voice gets too loud – spend a moment simply noticing them, without judgement, and reconnect with the silent awareness behind them. This is a place of true calm, and it is available to you whenever you wish to go there.

There is a voice that
doesn't use words.

Listen.

Rumi

SILENCE YOUR INNER CRITIC

Do you find it difficult to silence your inner critic? Meditation, exercise, reading and yoga can all help to press the mute button – try a few of these options to find what works for you. Everyone is different – you'll know you've found the perfect remedy when you start to feel peaceful and able to notice the silence within yourself.

YOU CAN'T CALM THE STORM, SO STOP TRYING. WHAT YOU CAN DO IS CALM YOURSELF. THE STORM WILL PASS.

Timber Hawkeye

OVERRIDE YOUR
CURRENT THINKING

Don't believe every thought you have. For example, the thought "I'm not good enough" is neither helpful nor true. When it pops into your head, take a moment to think of some examples that prove otherwise.

IF ONE'S MIND HAS PEACE, THE WHOLE WORLD WILL APPEAR PEACEFUL.

Ramana Maharshi

CULTIVATE A POSITIVE MINDSET

Do you find that phrases such as "I hate Mondays" are the first to pop into your head each day? If you've slowly spiralled into a pattern of negative thinking, it's time to start cultivating a more positive mindset. Start to challenge those negative thoughts, by reframing them in a more positive light. For example, do you really hate Mondays? It's likely that good things will happen during the day, such as that first sip of hot tea or lunch with a friend. Focus on these aspects, rather than making sweeping negative statements, and seek out positive news stories to give yourself a boost.

ALLOW YOURSELF TO ENJOY THIS DAY.

To experience peace does not mean that your life is always blissful. It means that you are capable of tapping into a blissful state of mind amidst the normal chaos of a hectic life.

Jill Bolte Taylor

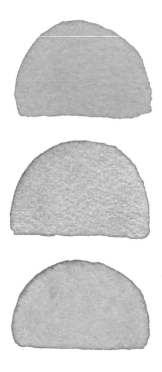

MAKE IT A HABIT

The more you override negative thought patterns, the easier it will become. Of course, we all go through difficult periods in life, but over time, you will find it easier to adopt a positive mindset in the face of adversity.

Relax and Unwind

MAKE TIME FOR SIMPLE PLEASURES

Scattering each day with small moments that make you happy is a fantastic way to escape stress. From using a zingy and refreshing shower gel, to wearing your favourite jumper, do something that puts a smile on your face.

Look deep into nature, and then you will understand everything better.

Albert Einstein

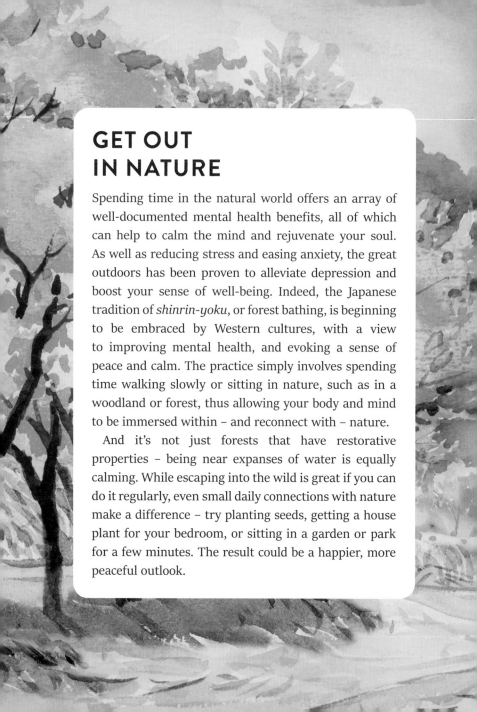

GET OUT IN NATURE

Spending time in the natural world offers an array of well-documented mental health benefits, all of which can help to calm the mind and rejuvenate your soul. As well as reducing stress and easing anxiety, the great outdoors has been proven to alleviate depression and boost your sense of well-being. Indeed, the Japanese tradition of *shinrin-yoku*, or forest bathing, is beginning to be embraced by Western cultures, with a view to improving mental health, and evoking a sense of peace and calm. The practice simply involves spending time walking slowly or sitting in nature, such as in a woodland or forest, thus allowing your body and mind to be immersed within – and reconnect with – nature.

And it's not just forests that have restorative properties – being near expanses of water is equally calming. While escaping into the wild is great if you can do it regularly, even small daily connections with nature make a difference – try planting seeds, getting a house plant for your bedroom, or sitting in a garden or park for a few minutes. The result could be a happier, more peaceful outlook.

RIVERS KNOW THIS: THERE IS NO HURRY. WE SHALL GET THERE SOME DAY.

A. A. Milne

Nothing in nature blooms all year round.

HEAD FOR A WALK

Walking can do wonders for your mental well-being – in fact, regular walks are proven to improve your self-esteem and overall mood, as well as lowering stress, anxiety, fatigue and depression. Try a gentle stroll to calm your soul.

Adopt the pace of nature:

her secret is patience.

Ralph Waldo Emerson

HAVE A LONG
SOAK IN THE BATH

Slipping into a warm bath at the end of a long
day is wonderfully restorative and peaceful. Add
your favourite aromatherapy oil or bubbles and light
some scented candles for an extra dose of calm.

Soak up Serenity.

SIP A CUP OF HOT TEA

There's an excellent reason why many of us love to sit down and slowly savour a mug of our favourite tea: studies have shown that tea drinking can have a similar effect on the brain as meditation, stimulating the alpha brainwaves associated with relaxation and mental clarity. In fact, in the 1100s, formal Zen Buddhist tea-drinking ceremonies were created purely with the aim of aiding meditation. There are so many different varieties of tea to choose from, so why not experiment a little? Both black and green teas contain high levels of the amino acid L-Theanine, known to increase dopamine levels, which can help to induce a wonderfully calming state. Or try soothing camomile, which has been shown to reduce stress and anxiety, as well as relaxing muscle tension.

A cup of tea
is a cup of peace.

Sen Sōshitsu XV

GET LOST IN A GOOD BOOK

There's nothing like curling up on the sofa with a page-turning
novel to help you feel calm. Indeed, studies have shown
that reading can help to reduce stress levels. So go on – dive
into a new or favourite book and get lost in its story.

MINIMIZE SCREEN TIME

Studies show that excessive screen time equals a decrease in real-life human interaction, which can result in increased anxiety and feelings of isolation. When in the company of others, keep your phone out of reach, so you can engage fully with the people around you.

Freedom from desire leads to inner peace.

Lao Tzu

**LET GO OF ANY EXPECTATIONS
YOU MAY HAVE OF YOURSELF,
EVEN IF IT'S JUST FOR A MOMENT.**

HAVE A SOCIAL MEDIA DETOX

Constantly checking online social platforms can be potentially damaging to your self-esteem, and leave you feeling more lonely and anxious. So have a detox, even just for one day each week, to reconnect with both yourself and others in a more genuine and compassionate way.

**ALMOST EVERYTHING WILL
WORK AGAIN IF YOU UNPLUG
IT FOR A FEW MINUTES,**

INCLUDING YOU.

Anne Lamott

DECLUTTER YOUR PHYSICAL SPACE

Clinging on to lots of unnecessary possessions, and being constantly confronted with cluttered surfaces and cramped cupboards, is a sure-fire path to stress within the home. Getting rid of unwanted items can be a highly cathartic process, ultimately leaving you with a clutter-free, minimalistic living space that will help to promote a sense of calm. If you're the sort of person who holds on to loads of stuff, the prospect of clearing it out can seem overwhelming. It's a good idea to break the process down to make it more manageable. Start with just one cupboard – or even just one drawer. Set aside a morning (or even 10 minutes) and get clearing, working through a new area of your home every chance you get. It will soon add up! Rather than chucking everything into the bin, decide what could be taken to a charity shop or donated to a local cause. The added feel-good factor from doing something worthwhile is bound to boost your mood.

THE BEST WAY TO FIND OUT WHAT WE REALLY NEED IS TO GET RID OF WHAT WE DON'T.

Marie Kondo

CREATE A TO-DO LIST

Writing down everything you need to get done each day, and then crossing it off the list once completed, can help you to feel less chaotic and more in control, as well as providing evidence of all you've achieved that day. Be realistic, though, to make sure you don't overload yourself.

It's not about having it all.

It's about having what you value most.

Jean Chatzky

ORGANIZE YOUR
TIME EFFECTIVELY

Nothing is more likely to leave you stressed and anxious than feeling
as if you're constantly late or running out of time. Getting on top
of tasks by managing your time more effectively can help you to
experience more calm and peace in your day-to-day life. Think about
a particular aspect of your day where you always seem to feel pressed
for time, such as getting ready for work. How could you streamline
your morning to ensure you aren't rushing around? For example,
could you pack your bag, lay your clothes out and even prep your
breakfast (overnight oats can be stored in the fridge in readiness) the
evening before? This could leave you with an extra 20 minutes each
morning, during which you could integrate a calming practice, such
as a short meditation, to start your day with a positive intention.

YOUR INNER PEACE IS YOUR MOST VALUABLE TREASURE.

GET ON TOP OF YOUR FINANCES

Money worries are a common cause of anxiety. Facing your financial fears head-on will help. Seek advice on how to manage your money, prioritize any debts you may have and start paying them off, even if it's just a little bit at a time. The sooner you begin to take positive action, the better for your peace of mind (as well as your credit score).

Beware of little expenses.
A small leak will
sink a great ship.

Benjamin Franklin

OPEN

ARMS.

OPEN

MIND.

OPEN

HEART.

HUG A
LOVED ONE

Physical contact is scientifically
proven to lower blood pressure and
boost levels of oxytocin (the "love
hormone") in the body. A quick hug
from a loved one or friend could
be a great calming influence.

HAVE A LAUGH

Laughter can be the perfect antidote to a stressful day, relaxing the body and releasing feel-good hormones to create a natural high. Try watching a TV comedy or listening to a funny podcast, and enjoy a good belly laugh!

smile more worry less.

TRY MINDFUL COLOURING

Colouring is a wonderful way to unwind. There are plenty of adult colouring books available to help you become more mindful as you find your creative groove, so pick up those pencils and rediscover a childhood love.

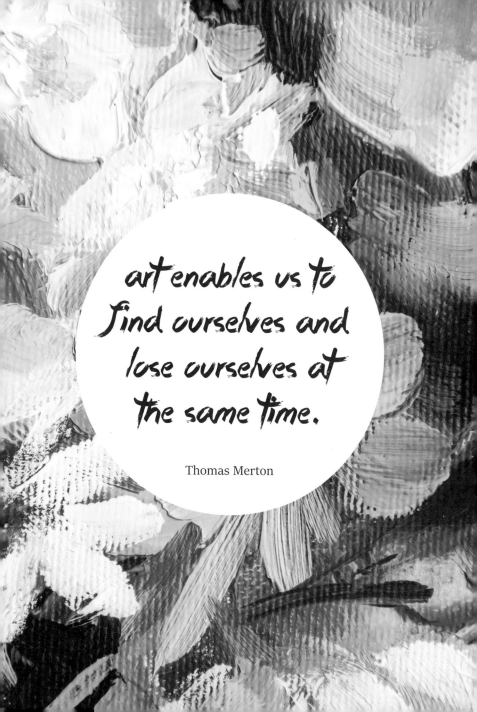

art enables us to
find ourselves and
lose ourselves at
the same time.

Thomas Merton

GET CREATIVE

Throwing yourself into a creative project can be deeply satisfying, and focusing all of your mindful attention onto making, creating or designing can soothe and calm your busy mind. Creativity can take many forms: from painting, drawing, colouring and sculpting, through to sewing, knitting, baking, writing, singing, dancing or acting. There are numerous studies which demonstrate that tapping into our creative side does wonders for our mental health, so choose a pursuit that appeals to you and get stuck in. The good news is that you don't have to be an expert in your chosen field – the joy lies in the creative act itself, as opposed to the finished outcome. So let loose and create – and embrace the accompanying inner joy and peace.

What art
offers is
space —
a certain
breathing
room for
the spirit.

John Updike

TRY "EARTHING"

Spending time barefoot can be incredibly grounding. Try going barefoot each time you stand in your garden, or when you visit a park or beach. Visualize yourself connecting with the earth and imagine any stress melting away.

I AM A PART OF
NATURE AND NATURE
IS A PART OF ME.

RECHARGE FOR
A WHOLE DAY

Having an entire day to yourself to focus on your own well-being may feel self-indulgent, but think about how many people would appreciate a calmer, happier, recharged you. If you have a family, you might feel guilty about taking so much time just for yourself, but carving out a day of solitude will enable you to rebalance both your body and mind, leaving you feeling more peaceful and better able to deal with whatever life has in store. Speak with those close to you if you think it would help to ensure they understand why it's important. Then plan your day! Think about things you love doing and activities that will help you to unwind. Read a good book, make a delicious lunch, curl up on the sofa and watch your favourite movie, head for a gentle stroll, soak in a long bath... The day is yours, so do as you see fit to help calm your body, mind and soul.

Know
that you
are loved.

Sometimes, the most
productive thing you
can do is relax.

Mark Black

STRETCH IT OUT

When you're stressed, your muscles tend to tense up, which can make you feel even worse. Several times a day, spend a few minutes stretching out any physical tension to ease both your body and mind.

LOOK UP

If you're feeling overwhelmed, take a moment to step outside and look up. What can you see? Perhaps it's buildings – homes, office blocks, monuments or skyscrapers – rising up from the ground where you stand; maybe it's treetops, an interlacing of leaves and branches. What then? Can you see sky? Is it cloudy? Sunny? Take a moment to breathe in the ever-expanding space above you. Taking a short while to appreciate the vastness of the sky can sometimes put our own issues or problems into perspective, making us realize they are perhaps not as significant as we thought they were.

LET CALMNESS BLOOM

A bunch of flowers can really brighten a dreary day. Studies have also found that being able to see flowers helps people to feel less anxious. So that pretty bouquet really does promote calmness! Keep your flowers close by and gaze upon them mindfully every time you desire a dose of beautiful peace.

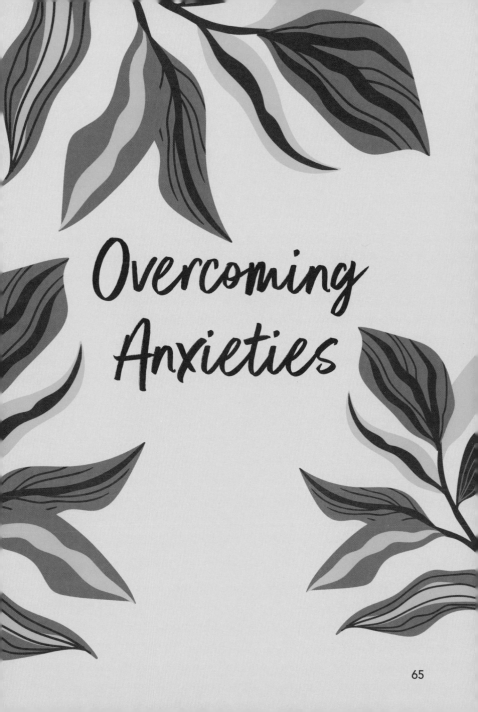

Overcoming Anxieties

TAKE A MOMENT
TO PAUSE

Whenever you start feeling overwhelmed,
stop what you're doing for a short
moment. Focus on a physical object
within your vicinity and notice three
facts about it. Distracting your mind like
this is an easy way to promote calm.

Breath is the power
behind all things. I breathe
in and know that good
things will happen.

Tao Porchon-Lynch

BREATHE
MORE DEEPLY

Taking a few deep breaths really does promote inner peace. Scientific research has now found that lengthening the breath triggers neurons in your brain that tell your body it's time to relax. This type of deep, conscious breathing – also known as diaphragmatic breathing – is a quick and easy technique to help relieve any anxiety or stress you may be feeling. What's more, the beauty of breathwork is that it can be done virtually anywhere and you don't need lots of time. To begin, ensure you're sitting comfortably; then start to breathe consciously, focusing on elongating each inhale through your nose, feeling your belly expand and rise, and then exhaling through your mouth for slightly longer. Perhaps breathe in for a count of four and then out for a count of five. Still your mind and focus on each slow, deliberate breath.

If you want
to conquer
the anxiety of
life, live in the
moment, live
in the breath.

Amit Ray

Keep calm

and

breathe deeply.

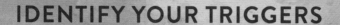

IDENTIFY YOUR TRIGGERS

Spend a little time identifying the cause (or causes) of your anxiety – is it large crowds, fear of failure, financial issues or a past trauma? Knowing your triggers can help you to manage them, which can promote a sense of control.

FACE YOUR FEARS

It can be hard to adopt a calm demeanour if you're hiding fears, worries or anxieties just below the surface. Confronting your fears can seem scary, but you will most likely find that bringing them into the light, examining them and then taking measures to deal with them will actually remove any power they have previously held over you.

So spend a little time confronting your fears – it might be painful, but dealing with them will help you to achieve long-term inner peace. Write down the things that are bothering you, followed by some steps that you could take to overcome them. Is it something you can start to deal with alone? Would it help to open up to a friend or partner? Might it be a good idea to seek professional help, such as a therapist? By actively attempting to overcome the things that scare you, their significance will begin to fade.

It seems to me that
the less I fight my fear,
the less it fights back.
If I can relax,
fear relaxes, too.

Elizabeth Gilbert

EVERYTHING IS
GOING TO BE OK.

CONSIDER THE WORST-CASE SCENARIO

If you're experiencing stress, confronting the worst possible outcome could help you to move beyond the anxiety you're feeling. Once we dissect the worst-case scenario and realize that, even if it happened, we would cope, a sense of control and calm is restored. For example, let's consider the worst-case scenario of a big work presentation: you might forget your facts and figures, which could cause embarrassment for your company, which could mean you lose your job, which could mean you risk being unable to pay your rent, which could mean you have to move in with a family member for a while. But if all that were to happen, would you still, deep down, be OK? Would you still be you? Would you still be able to come up with a solution? Realizing that you will be fine, even if your worst-case scenario plays out, is very grounding.

PEACE IS THE RESULT OF RETRAINING YOUR MIND TO PROCESS LIFE AS IT IS, RATHER THAN AS YOU THINK IT SHOULD BE.

Wayne W. Dyer

ACCEPT THAT LIFE IS UNCERTAIN

Uncertainty can make us feel vulnerable. However, being able to let go and embrace the uncertainty of life is a liberating experience. Accepting that it's OK to not know what lies ahead can free you up to feel more at peace.

LEARN TO RATIONALIZE

It can be easy to let anxieties spiral out of control at an alarming rate. If you notice this happening, take a moment to stop – then look at the situation with a clear head. By examining any irrational thoughts you may have, using your calm and rational mind, you should be able to ease any worries and come up with a more positive way forward. Once you start picking your anxiety apart, you are likely to realize that the thing you are most scared of happening is actually not likely to happen at all.

STOP AIMING
FOR PERFECTION

The fear of imperfection can not only create
anxiety, but also stop you moving forward
or trying something new, in case you make a
mistake. Realize that perfection is an illusion,
and that "good enough" truly is good enough.

LIST THE
POSITIVES

By writing down everything positive in your life –
even seemingly insignificant details – you will gain
perspective when you feel stressed or unhappy.
While you might be dealing with a difficult situation
right now, there are bound to be blessings aplenty
to appreciate, if you just let yourself look for them.

The present moment is filled with joy and happiness. If you are attentive, you will see it.

Thích Nhất Hạnh

RECOGNIZE THE MOMENTS WHEN YOU'RE DOING FINE

Spend a day becoming consciously aware of all the times you feel OK. When dealing with stress and anxiety, you often focus on the moments when you feel overwhelmed – so much so that the times you are doing fine get overlooked.

Find strength in inner peace.

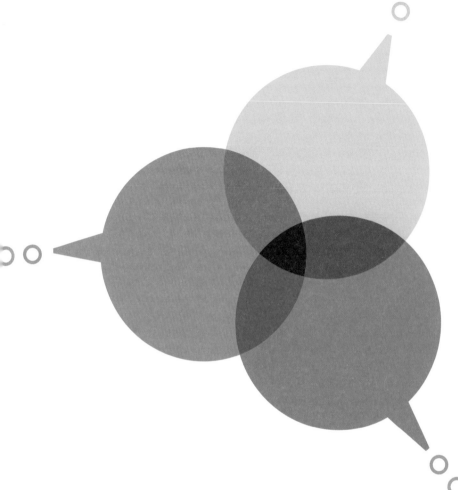

NOTICE YOUR THOUGHTS,
WITHOUT JUDGEMENT...

Becoming aware of thought patterns is the first step to
changing them. When negative thoughts arise, simply sit with
them for a moment. Don't buy into them or change them –
simply notice what your internal voice is saying.

... AND THEN
CHALLENGE THEM

Once you've noticed negative thoughts, take each one and question its validity. Is there evidence for it? Would a friend say this to or about you? Realizing many negative thoughts are irrational can help to restore your inner calm.

YOUR GOAL IS NOT TO BATTLE WITH THE MIND, BUT TO WITNESS THE MIND.

Swami Muktananda

Mistakes happen.

Forgive yourself.

Staying
Healthy

DRINK MORE WATER

Dehydration is linked to poor mental health and decreased cognitive function, so drinking water is an easy way to protect your peace of mind. Aim for six to eight glasses daily – add natural flavour with lemon, cucumber or mint leaves, if you like.

The body is your temple. Keep it pure and clean for the soul to reside in.

B. K. S. Iyengar

CUT BACK ON ALCOHOL

Alcohol is a depressant that can negatively impact your thoughts, feelings, emotions and sleep quality. Cutting back as much as possible is a brilliant way to benefit your long-term mental health and inner peace. Try a booze-free week as a first step.

BODY, YOU'LL THANK ME LATER.

EAT MORE
FRUIT AND VEG

Boosting your intake of colourful fruits and vegetables is fabulous for your body and mind. Aim for five a day and try to eat seasonally: think berries and salads in summer, followed by apples, root veg and squashes as the seasons change. Fuelling yourself with the vitamins and minerals you need is an easy way to ensure balance and good health – for body, mind and soul.

EAT GOOD FATS

Fat in your diet is necessary for good health. Certain fats, such as the polyunsaturated and monounsaturated varieties, are vital for healthy brain function and can even help to regulate feelings of stress. So stock up on oily fish, nuts, olives, olive oil and avocados to give your body what it needs to run smoothly. Keep red meat, butter and cheese to a minimum.

Be kind to yourself.

COOKING IS AT ONCE
CHILD'S PLAY AND ADULT JOY.
AND COOKING DONE WITH
CARE IS AN ACT OF LOVE.

Craig Claiborne

DON'T REACH FOR PROCESSED FOODS

Find comfort in home-made dishes, like hearty stews and soups, instead of reaching for shop-bought baked goods and processed snacks. The latter are packed with excess sugar and trans fats, which are bad for your body and can make you feel sluggish.

COOK HEALTHY MEALS FROM SCRATCH

Creating a delicious plateful of food made from lovingly chosen ingredients is not only a wonderful way to nourish your body, but it is also a powerful act of self-care that's good for your mind and soul. Have a think about the type of healthy foods that bring a smile to your face. If you don't normally spend much time preparing meals in the kitchen, opting for simple recipes is a great start to help you build both confidence and skill. Good options include hearty one-pot stews, flavoursome soups or rainbow salads.

Search through cookbooks for inspiration, ensure you have all the necessary ingredients and then get cooking! Make sure you have plenty of time, and take it step by step: following a recipe is a great way of staying in the present moment – many people find it a wholly relaxing, mindful practice. And the best bit? The end result will be a delicious, wholesome meal to enjoy. Don't worry if it doesn't go quite right first time – the joy of cooking is in the experiment and discovery!

MAKE TIME
FOR FITNESS

A regular exercise routine is one of the best ways to help calm a frazzled mind. Numerous studies have shown that physical exercise that raises your heart rate is proven to reduce stress, alleviate anxiety and even ease mild to moderate depression. In fact, many health professionals now prescribe physical activity to patients suffering with poor mental health. Anecdotal evidence also abounds: people report feeling happier, calmer and more relaxed following a fitness session – thought to be due to the endorphins ("feel-good" hormones) that are released into the bloodstream during exercise.

You may feel you can't fit exercise into your already packed schedule, but carving out time to care for your physical and mental health is one of the most positive steps you can take to help improve your well-being. Go through your diary and write in times when you could get active. It doesn't have to be for a long duration, especially if you're new to exercise – even just 10 or 20 minutes is a good start, and it all adds up. Remember: brisk walking counts, too, so try short distances, picking your pace up to get your heart racing.

EXER CISE

is nature's

ANTIDEPRESSANT.

FIND EXERCISE
YOU ENJOY

Hate the gym? Then you're unlikely to stick with it. Choosing a fitness pursuit you love is key. From swimming or jogging, to climbing, dancing, cycling and kayaking, there's an option for everyone. Don't quit until you find it.

Being still does
not mean don't move.
It means move in peace.

E'yen A. Gardner

FOCUS ON ALL THAT YOU ARE, INSTEAD OF ALL THAT YOU ARE NOT.

TRY YOGA

Yoga is a spiritual practice that blends a series of postures (asanas) with breathing and meditation. This helps to evoke a sense of calm, peace and stillness within, as well as creating balance in the body, and improving both mental and physical strength. The word "yoga" is rooted in the Sanskrit *yui*, meaning "to unite", and you will likely experience a sense of harmony between your mind, body and soul as you begin your yoga journey. While you have the option of practising it in the comfort of your own home, if you're new to yoga it's a good idea to seek out a class led by a fully qualified instructor, who will be able to gently guide you through the poses.

YOGA IS
NOT ABOUT
TOUCHING
YOUR TOES.
IT IS WHAT
YOU LEARN
ON THE
WAY DOWN.

Jigar Gor

GET SOME SUNSHINE

Spending time outside in the sunlight can be a wonderful mood booster – and it's actually important for your health, too. Vitamin D (produced by your body when your skin is exposed to direct sunlight) is vital for healthy bones, teeth, muscles and immunity. Scientists also believe there is a link between vitamin D and your mental health, with low levels of the vitamin associated with depression and seasonal affective disorder (SAD). Try to get outside as often as you can and soak up some "happy" rays to ease and calm your mind. In winter months, when the sun is too low in the sky for your body to make adequate levels of vitamin D, a supplement can be beneficial.

Inner
stillness
is the key
to outer
strength.

Jared Brock

TAKE A NAP

A short snooze of 20–30 minutes can aid relaxation, boost your mood, reduce fatigue and increase alertness, all of which play a part in creating a calmer state of mind. Closing your eyes and switching off for a short while will help you to approach the rest of your day with a more peaceful demeanour.

Finish each day before you begin the next, and interpose a solid wall of sleep between the two.

Ralph Waldo Emerson

CREATE A
BEDTIME ROUTINE

Often, we feel we have so much to fit into our day that we end up
working or completing household chores right up until bedtime.
But by trying to squeeze as much out of each day as possible,
we're leaving little room for relaxation and calm. If you can, try
to carve out at least 30–60 minutes before bed, and use this
purely as time to decelerate and unwind from your day.

You could read, take a bath, stretch, try some gentle yoga poses or perform a breathing meditation. The idea is to slow your thoughts in preparation for sleep. Getting into a routine, by performing your own relaxing bedtime ritual on a regular basis, will help to signal to your body that it's time for sleep, thus ensuring that you are well rested and focused the following day.

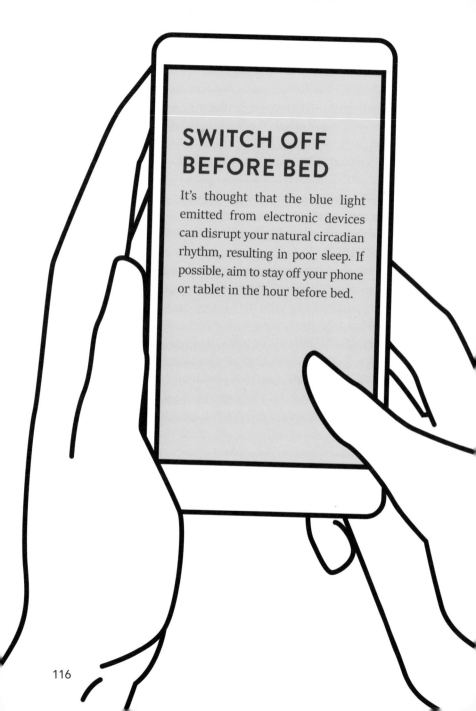

SWITCH OFF BEFORE BED

It's thought that the blue light emitted from electronic devices can disrupt your natural circadian rhythm, resulting in poor sleep. If possible, aim to stay off your phone or tablet in the hour before bed.

ALLOW YOURSELF TIME TO RECHARGE.

GET MORE SLEEP

Studies have shown that sleep deprivation is bad for both your mental and physical health, resulting in impaired memory, poor attention span and flattened emotional responses, as well as an increased risk of developing high blood pressure and heart disease. So getting enough sleep each night is vital, in order to feel calm, healthy and alert each day. Guidelines recommend that, as adults, we need roughly 8 hours of sleep each night, although you may need to spend a little longer in bed in order to achieve this – perhaps 9 hours.

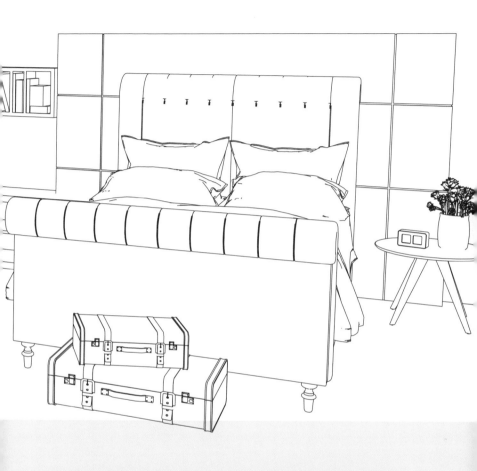

To better aid a good night's sleep, make sure your bedroom environment is just right: try to maintain a room temperature of 16–18°C, ensure it's dark at night (try a blackout blind or eye mask if street lighting is a problem), make sure your mattress is comfortable and aim to keep noise to a minimum – earplugs can be a life-saver if you happen to live in an area where there are frequent disruptions, such as traffic noise.

Promoting Inner Calm

SLOWLY
COUNT TO TEN

If you feel overwhelmed, angry or stressed, counting to ten can be an effective way of calming your mind, as well as giving you the space and time to decide how to move forward in any situation. Counting slowly, perhaps matching the rhythm to your breath, is the perfect way to press pause in times of tension.

TRY VISUALIZATION

Visualization can be a powerful relaxation technique, which works by using mental imagery to help focus and calm your mind. It can work well to combat stress and anxiety, by taking your mind off any negative thoughts. To begin, set aside 10 or 15 minutes when you can sit quietly by yourself. Once you've made sure you're comfortable, gently close your eyes and take a few deep breaths to help still your mind. Then visualize a calming scene. It could be a deserted beach, a mountain view or a flower-filled meadow – wherever most appeals to you.

Let's take the meadow example: start to imagine a crisp blue sky above you, as you slowly walk through the swaying grass. You notice a soft picnic blanket laid out in front of you, and you walk over and lie down. You are surrounded by beautiful flowers and can hear the swish of the grass blown by a gentle breeze. You are perfectly warm and relaxed. What else can you see, hear and feel? Notice the tension dropping from your face and shoulders. Take time to relish the peace. When you're ready, slowly bring your mind back to the present moment.

Inhale slowly,

EXHALE
DEEPLY.

Meditation is a way for nourishing and blossoming the divinity within you.

Amit Ray

MEDITATE DAILY

Performing a daily meditation is a wonderfully calming ritual. In fact, studies have found that it can have powerful positive effects on both your body and mind, including lowering heart rate and blood pressure, improving circulation, reducing stress and boosting overall well-being. There are many different forms of meditation. Some focus on following your breath, while others involve directing your attention on an external object, such as a candle flame or crystal. Essentially, though, all meditation is focused attention.

To begin, ensure you're sitting comfortably, with your back straight and upright, and your eyes gently closed, if you wish. Whichever form of meditation you decide on, attempt to clear your mind of everything else. If you notice thoughts creeping in, gently draw your attention back to your breath (or the object you're focusing on), without judgement or guilt. Aim for just 10 minutes at first – even a short session can soothe your mind.

YOU MUST LEARN TO LET GO. RELEASE THE STRESS. YOU WERE NEVER IN CONTROL ANYWAY.

Steve Maraboli

Stop waiting for the future... live in the present.

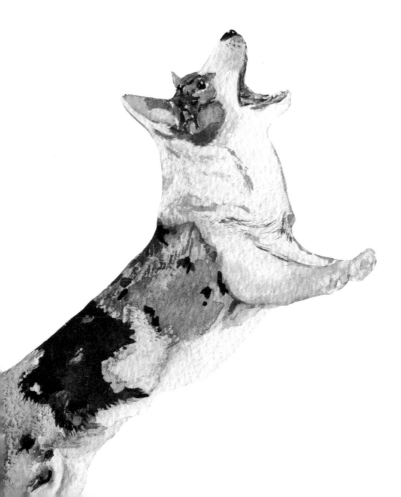

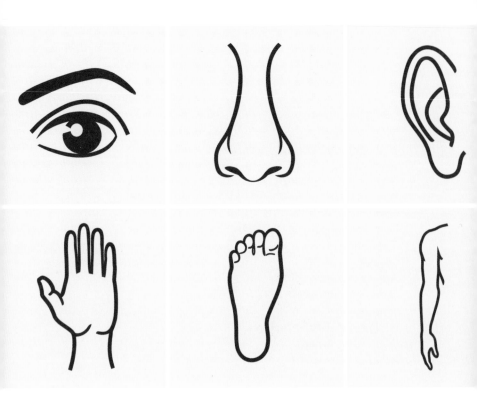

PERFORM A BODY SCAN

A body-scan meditation is a calming way to become fully aware of your physical self in the present moment and, while relaxation is not the end goal, it's a common side effect. To start, sit or lie in a comfortable position, ensuring that your clothing isn't tight or constricting. You may want to remove any heavy jewellery. Take a few deep breaths and then slowly bring your awareness to your feet: pay attention to their position on the floor, whether they feel warm or cool and whether they feel tense or relaxed. The aim is not to change, but simply to notice.

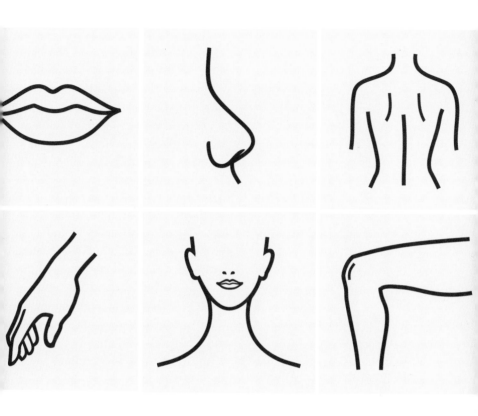

Move your awareness slowly up through your body: to your calves, knees, thighs, buttocks, hips, pelvis, lower back, stomach, chest, upper back, shoulders, arms, hands, fingers, neck, jaw, cheeks, eyes, forehead, temples and crown of the head, noticing how each part feels in that moment. Moving your awareness to your body and away from your thoughts is a grounding act and can instil a sense of peace.

The best cure for the body is a quiet mind.

Napoleon Bonaparte

LISTEN TO MUSIC

Music can have a profound impact on your mind and body, with slower tempos helping to ease stress, release tension and reduce anxiety. Try creating a soothing playlist to listen to whenever you need to restore a sense of peace.

CHOOSE HOW
YOU RESPOND

Have you ever considered the difference between a reaction and a response? The former is usually instantaneous and often comes from a place of uncertainty, pressure, anger, anxiety or fear. A response, on the other hand, comes from a place of conscious consideration. When something happens that annoys, upsets or angers you, notice and honour that emotion, but before acting on it, wait a moment.

Ponder the situation. What else is going on? Why has this happened? If someone else is involved, are they hurt, upset or confused? Pausing, breathing and taking a moment to consider each situation can help you to avoid fractious reactions, so that you can respond from a place of calm.

A CONSIDERED RESPONSE DEMONSTRATES STRENGTH.

*I can have peace of mind only when
I forgive rather than judge.*

Gerald Jampolsky

THE LESS YOU REACT TO DRAMA,

the more peaceful life becomes.

REALIZE THAT
DIFFICULTIES WILL PASS

Challenges, difficulties and tough times are all part of life. Accepting this, as well as adopting an understanding that they will eventually pass, is a wonderful way of maintaining your peace of mind, even

*Loss is nothing else but change,
and change is nature's delight.*

Marcus Aurelius

LET YOUR GRATITUDE GROW

Spending a little time each day expressing gratitude does so much more than increase your appreciation for the good things in your life (although that's obviously a great side effect). Research has found that gratitude has a positive impact on almost all aspects of life, including increasing optimism, improving self-esteem, strengthening relationships, deepening relaxation, boosting energy, improving sleep, promoting kindness and enhancing spirituality. In short, expressing gratitude makes you happier!

A good way to begin is to start keeping a daily gratitude journal – you don't have to write lots (although, of course, you can if you wish). Perhaps start by listing the three things you feel most grateful for at the end of each day. After a month, notice how this practice has changed your outlook. Many people report increased positivity, which can enhance feelings of inner peace.

There is a calmness to a life lived
in gratitude, a quiet joy.

Ralph H. Blum

Silence is strength.

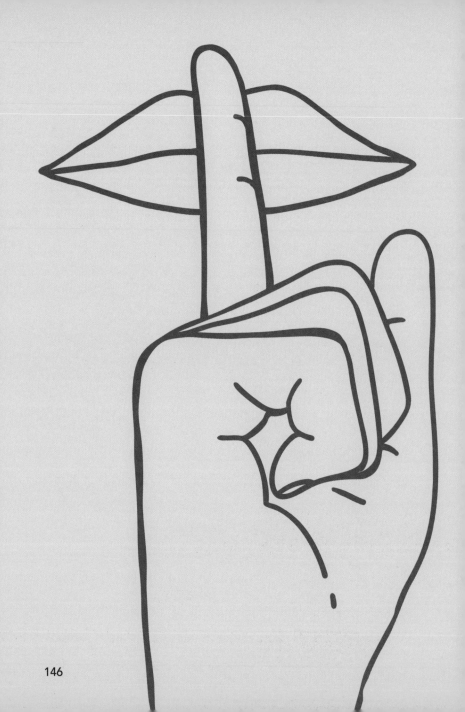

EMBRACE SILENCE

A little quiet time could be the key not just to a calm mind, but also to a host of additional well-being benefits. According to research into changes in blood pressure, silence can help to relieve stress and tension in as little as 2 minutes, providing greater relaxation than listening to soothing music. Silence can also stimulate brain cell growth, boost memory and improve sleep quality. So if you're feeling overwhelmed, spend a few minutes sitting comfortably in silence; don't forget to switch off any background noise or electronic devices, so you won't get disturbed. Alternatively, head for a walk in nature and embrace the quiet outdoor space.

True silence is the
rest of the mind,
and is to the spirit
what sleep is to the
body, nourishment
and refreshment.

William Penn

SPEND TIME ALONE

A little solitude can do wonders for your mental health. In the moments you have by yourself, spend time doing something you love – read, write, paint, practise yoga, meditate – and enjoy the peace it brings.

Within you, there is a stillness and sanctuary to which you can retreat at any time and be yourself.

Hermann Hesse

FOCUS ON
YOUR STRENGTHS

Paying attention to the things you are good at, rather than highlighting your areas of weakness, is an empowering act and one that can leave you feeling stronger, more focused and calm. Concentrate on the strengths you bring to any and every situation.

YOU ARE STRONGER THAN YOU THINK.

The real meditation is how you live your life.

Jon Kabat-Zinn

BE KIND

Being kind is a positive and powerful way to boost feelings of well-being in both you and those around you; it has been scientifically proven to help you feel happier and more relaxed, by increasing levels of the hormone dopamine in your body. What's more, being kind is actually good for your health – studies have found that performing acts of kindness may help to lower the risk of cardiovascular disease, regulate glucose levels and even play a part in your immune response. Aim to do at least one kind act each day: from hugging a loved one, smiling at a stranger or holding a door open for someone, to volunteering for a local charity, donating to a food bank or picking up litter. Pay attention to how you feel as the days go on – brightening someone else's day is likely to brighten yours as well.

DON'T LET PEOPLE PULL YOU INTO THEIR STORM.

PULL THEM INTO YOUR PEACE.

Kimberly Jones

NOTICE THE
BIGGER PICTURE

Worry and anxiety often result in a loss of perspective.
Try to see the bigger picture: will this situation affect
you next month? Next year? In five years? Zooming
out can be a powerful way to calm your mind.

Worry pretends to be necessary but serves no useful purpose.

Eckhart Tolle

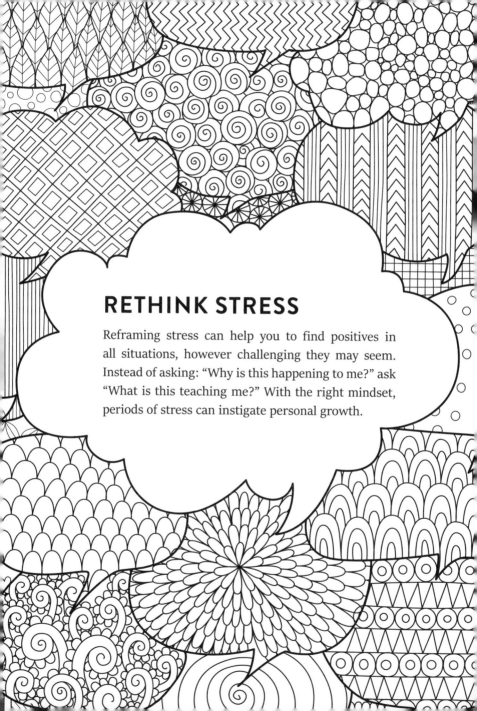

RETHINK STRESS

Reframing stress can help you to find positives in all situations, however challenging they may seem. Instead of asking: "Why is this happening to me?" ask "What is this teaching me?" With the right mindset, periods of stress can instigate personal growth.

Happiness is when what you think, what you say, and what you do are in harmony.

Mahatma Gandhi

CREATE POSITIVE AFFIRMATIONS

Repeating a positive affirmation each morning can help you to start the day feeling balanced and in control. Choose a phrase that resonates with you and sets a peaceful tone, such as: "I inhale calmness and exhale tension."

Don't let worry rob you of happiness.

IN THE MIDST
OF MOVEMENT
AND CHAOS,
KEEP STILLNESS
INSIDE OF YOU.

Deepak Chopra

SLOW DOWN

Rushing through the day, whether you're walking fast or ploughing through your inbox, can create anxiety. To counteract this, aim to consciously slow down your actions. You'll be amazed how this simple act can instantly promote a feeling of calm.

Nature does not hurry, yet everything is accomplished.

Lao Tzu

Therapies and Treatments

Grey skies are just
clouds passing over.

Duke Ellington

ASKING FOR HELP

Sometimes, it feels like you could invest in all the self-care in the world and yet still feel low, emotionally numb or disconnected from others. If you feel like you're experiencing depression or another serious mental health issue, it's important to open up to those close to you, if you are able, and to visit a health professional, who will listen to you and help you to choose the best course of action. Most importantly, please know that you are not alone: one in four adults experiences mental health issues at some point in their lives. Acknowledging that you need help can be difficult, but it's important to address how you are feeling, in order to begin to overcome any challenges in your path.

169

ACCESSING SUPPORT AND TREATMENT

If you are beginning to feel overwhelmed or unable to manage your stress alone, there is no shame in asking for help. In fact, making an appointment to speak with a professional, such as your doctor, shows strength and courage. You will be given the space to talk about the way you have been feeling in a safe and confidential environment. Opening up in this way is often a relief, especially if you've been struggling for a while.

COGNITIVE BEHAVIOURAL THERAPY

Cognitive behavioural therapy (CBT) is an effective talking therapy that can help you to manage and make sense of problems, by breaking them down into smaller, more manageable parts. Unlike other talking therapies, which often focus on your past, CBT encourages you to focus on the present moment and challenge any negative thought patterns you may be experiencing, in order to help you develop ways to change them. It is most commonly used to alleviate depression and anxiety – it's worth considering if you often feel very low or overwhelmed by worries.

It's never too late
to start afresh.

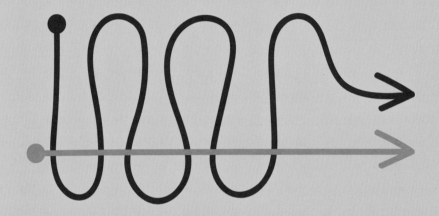

LIFE COACHING

Life coaching can help you to address a particular project or problem within your life; it is especially useful for those going through a transition period, whether that's returning to work after a long absence, a career change or something arising from your personal life. A life coach is a good expert to turn to if you would like to discover your values and unique purpose in life, and you will then be able to map out how you wish to move forward. It may be that you already hold all the answers you need: a coach simply helps you to unlock them from within, in order to show you how to lead a fulfilling, meaningful and purposeful life.

Let go of the life you think you need.
Embrace the life you are living now.

THE GREATEST WEAPON
AGAINST STRESS IS OUR
ABILITY TO CHOOSE ONE
THOUGHT OVER ANOTHER.

William James

COUNSELLING

Counselling offers a safe and confidential space in which to talk through your emotional concerns with a trained and empathetic professional. By facing your worries openly, you can find ways to deal with them. It's a good option if you're suffering with a mental health problem, such as anxiety, but can also help to support you through a challenging time in your life, such as a bereavement or relationship break-up.

AROMATHERAPY

This alternative therapy uses essential oils – which can be added to a bath, inhaled or used in massage – to rebalance your body and mind. Lavender, ylang-ylang and camomile oils are known for their soothing, calming properties.

REIKI

Reiki is an alternative therapy that can be used to help release tension and stress from within the body. The term itself is derived from the Japanese words *rei* (meaning "universal") and *ki* (meaning "life energy"), and it is commonly referred to as energy healing. Reiki is said to involve the transfer of universal energy from the practitioner's palms to the patient's body and, while its effectiveness is hard to prove in scientific terms, many who have experienced it are convinced of its benefits.

Reiki is said to increase your life force energy, which in turn can improve your physical, mental and spiritual well-being, promote healing, aid relaxation, relieve stress, and invoke a feeling of deep peace and calm.

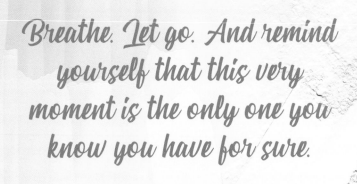

Breathe. Let go. And remind
yourself that this very
moment is the only one you
know you have for sure.

Oprah Winfrey

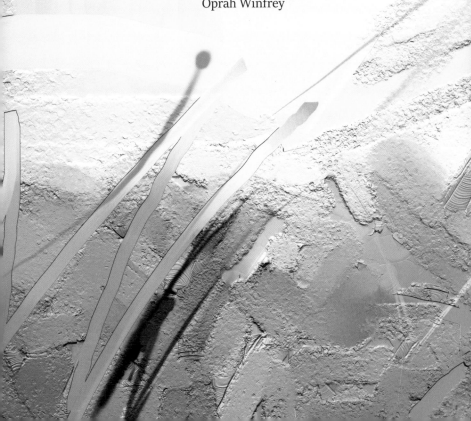

MASSAGE

As well as promoting a deep sense of relaxation, massage has been proven to ease stress, alleviate depression, soothe pain and release tension – perfect for calming your mind, body and soul. There are several different types of massage therapy: Swedish massage, for example, is a relaxing, full-body massage, while deep-tissue massage involves firmer pressure and is usually concentrated on a specific area to help relieve muscle tension. This can be a good option if you are experiencing physical pain due to stress.

It's always OK to ask for help.

HYPNOTHERAPY

Hypnotherapy is said to be useful in stopping repetitive negative thought patterns and altering unwanted habits, thus making it a valuable choice of therapy for those suffering with anxiety, stress or phobias. Sometimes people are nervous about hypnotherapy, but there's nothing to fear. After an initial chat, a trained hypnotherapist will lead you into a deeply relaxed state, before using the power of suggestion and imagination to alter your current thought patterns or behaviours. You remain conscious and in control throughout the process.

INNER PEACE BEGINS THE MOMENT
YOU CHOOSE NOT TO ALLOW
ANOTHER PERSON OR EVENT
TO CONTROL YOUR EMOTIONS.

Pema Chödrön

WALK-AND-TALK THERAPY

This "counselling in motion" takes traditional counselling practices out in the fresh air. Walking side by side while talking to a therapist can feel less intimidating than sitting face to face, while the open space also brings calming benefits. This type of therapy is becoming more widely available, as therapists are realizing the additional benefits of counselling in the open air – search online for a registered walk-and-talk practitioner in your area.

ART THERAPY

This expressive therapy uses creative processes, such as drawing, painting, colouring and sculpting, to aid self-expression and communication, and to examine any underlying psychological or emotional connotations within the artworks. It is used by professional art therapists as a way to address underlying emotional disruptions, and you don't need to be especially "creative" or have previous art experience to benefit. It's worth speaking to a mental health professional if you would like to find out more about accessing this type of therapy.

It's self-soothing for me to draw. So if I'm upset, drawing makes me less upset.

Bruce Eric Kaplan

YOU always have the POWER to choose YOUR OWN path.

CONCLUSION

In the midst of chronic stress or emotional turmoil, it can be difficult to believe that you will ever return to a sense of peacefulness. However, by accepting that your worries and negative thoughts are not true or permanent, and by adopting some of the calming self-care practices offered within these pages, you will see that – no matter how bad an external situation may seem – a feeling of inner peace is never far from reach. If you are able to, take a little time each day to look after your mind, body and soul – that sense of calm, happiness and positivity won't be far away.

Image credits

If you're interested in finding out more about our books, find us on Facebook at **Summersdale Publishers** and follow us on Twitter at **@Summersdale**.

www.summersdale.com